Unleashing the Power of TikTok: Discovering Innovative Ways to Generate Income on the Platform

Coloring Ape

Published by Coloring Ape, 2023.

While every precaution has been taken in the preparation of this book, the publisher assumes no responsibility for errors or omissions, or for damages resulting from the use of the information contained herein.

UNLEASHING THE POWER OF TIKTOK: DISCOVERING INNOVATIVE WAYS TO GENERATE INCOME ON THE PLATFORM

First edition. October 1, 2023.

Copyright © 2023 Coloring Ape.

ISBN: 979-8223910152

Written by Coloring Ape.

Also by Coloring Ape

Email Marketing Mastery: A Hands-On Approach for Small Business
Owners
Monetizing Your Passion: How to Turn Your Hobby into a Lucrative
Income Stream
Vegan Lifestyle for Pregnant Woman
Unleashing the Power of TikTok: Discovering Innovative Ways to
Generate Income on the Platform

Table of Contents

Unleashing the Power of TikTok: Discovering Innovative Ways to Generate Income on the Platform

In today's digital age, social media platforms have become an undeniable force, shaping the way we communicate, entertain ourselves, and even earn a living. Among the multitude of platforms available to users worldwide, TikTok has emerged as a ground-breaking platform that offers unique opportunities for individuals to generate income in innovative and creative ways. With its explosive growth and massive user base, harnessing the power of TikTok has become essential for those looking to capitalize on their talents or business ventures. In this article, we will explore how you can tap into this captivating platform's potential and discover groundbreaking methods to unleash your earning potential on TikTok. Join us as we delve into strategies employed by successful influencers and entrepreneurs who have cracked the code to monetizing their content effectively on TikTok – paving the way for a new era of financial success in the ever-evolving realm of social media. Get ready to unlock the limitless possibilities offered by TikTok and transform your passion into profit like never before!

Understanding the TikTok landscape: A brief overview

Understanding the TikTok Landscape: A Brief Overview

TikTok is a social media platform that allows users to create and share short videos. With over 2 billion downloads worldwide, it has quickly become one of the most popular apps among Gen Z and millennials.

The Power of Short-form Content

One of the reasons why TikTok has gained such immense popularity is its emphasis on short-form content. Users can create videos that are up to 60 seconds long, making it quick and easy for viewers to consume multiple videos in a single browsing session. This format caters perfectly to today's fast-paced digital environment, where attention spans are shorter than ever.

Building an Engaged Community

Another key aspect of TikTok is its strong sense of community. Users can follow accounts they find interesting or entertaining, and engage with them through comments and likes. This creates a sense of connection between creators and their audience, fostering loyalty and increasing engagement rates.

Overall, understanding the landscape of TikTok involves recognizing its focus on short-form content consumption as well as its ability to bring together creators and audiences in an engaged community setting. By tapping into these unique features, individuals have endless opportunities to generate income through innovative methods on this powerful platform.

Identifying your niche: Finding your unique selling point on TikTok

Identifying your niche: Finding your unique selling point on TikTok

Understand the platform

Before diving into creating content, it's crucial to understand what sets TikTok apart from other social media platforms. With its emphasis on short-form videos and engaging visuals, TikTok provides a unique opportunity for creators to showcase their talent, skills, or knowledge in an entertaining manner.

Research trends and popular content

To find your niche on TikTok, take some time to research trending topics and popular content within different niches. Look at what types of videos are attracting high engagement and resonating with the audience. This will give you insights into areas that have potential for growth.

Define your USP (Unique Selling Point)

Identify what makes you stand out from others who may be creating similar content. Whether it's a specific skillset, a distinct style of delivery, or expert knowledge in a particular subject matter—highlighting this unique aspect of yourself will help differentiate you from the crowd.

Experimentation is key

Don't be afraid to try new things and experiment with different types of content. Discover which format best showcases your talents while resonating with your target audience. By testing different approaches and analyzing viewer feedback through comments and metrics provided by the platform itself, you can refine your strategy over time.

Remember that building a successful presence on TikTok takes time; consistency is key here too! By discovering your niche and leveraging innovative ways to create compelling content that aligns with both brand values and user interests—that's when significant income-generating opportunities arise.

Building a strong TikTok presence: Strategies for gaining followers and engagement

- **Understand your target audience:** Before diving into TikTok, take the time to research and understand your target audience. What kind of content resonates with them? What hashtags do they engage with? By tailoring your content to their preferences, you can increase the likelihood of gaining followers and engagement.

- **Create high-quality videos:** In order to stand out on TikTok, it's important to create visually appealing and well-edited videos. Pay attention to factors like lighting, sound quality, and video resolution. This will help your content look professional and attract viewers.

- **Consistency is key:** To build a strong presence on TikTok, consistency is crucial. Regularly upload new content so that your followers have something fresh to engage with. Consider creating a posting schedule or using automated tools to ensure consistent activity without overwhelming yourself.

By following these strategies, you can set yourself up for success in building a strong TikTok presence. Remember that gaining followers and engagement takes time and effort, so be patient as you work towards growing your influence on the platform.

Creating captivating content: Tips for producing high-quality videos

Creating Captivating Content: Tips for Producing High-Quality Videos

For attracting attention on TikTok, high-quality videos are essential. Here are some tips to help you create captivating content that stands out:

- **Keep it short:** Shorter videos tend to perform better on TikTok. Aim for 15 seconds or less to keep viewers engaged and prevent boredom.

- **Grab attention from the start:** Start your video with a catchy hook or intriguing visual to instantly captivate your audience and encourage them to continue watching.

- **Use trendy music or sounds:** Music plays a significant role on TikTok, so choose popular songs or trendy sounds that fit well with your content. Utilize the platform's built-in library of music tracks or explore popular trends related to sound effects.

Making sure your videos stand out from the crowd doesn't have to be complicated. By keeping it short, grabbing attention quickly, and selecting engaging music, you'll be well on your way to creating high-quality content that captures viewers' interests and generates income on TikTok.

Leveraging TikTok trends: How to stay relevant and ride the wave

Understanding current TikTok trends is crucial for staying relevant on the platform. By keeping a close eye on popular challenges, dances, and memes, you can join in and create content that resonates with your audience.

Here are some tips for leveraging TikTok trends:

1. Observe and adapt: Spend time browsing through the "For You" page to see what types of content are trending. Look out for hashtags that are frequently used or popular sounds being used in videos. Adapt these trends to fit your unique style and niche.

2. Participate in challenges: Engage with existing viral challenges by creating your own version or adding a unique twist to stand out from others. Collaborating with other TikTokers who have already joined in on the challenge can help amplify your reach.

3. Stay consistent: Regularly post new content so you remain active within the TikTok community. Trends come and go quickly, so it's important to consistently engage with them while they're still hot.

Remember, authenticity is key when using TikTok trends as part of your income-generating strategy. Be true to yourself while putting your own spin on popular themes – this will give you a better chance of making an impact and building a loyal following.

Collaborating with influencers: Maximizing your reach and exposure

Partnering with influential TikTokers is a highly effective way to expand your reach and increase exposure on the platform.

1. Identify relevant influencers: Research popular accounts that align with your niche or target audience. Look for TikTok creators who have a large following and regularly engage with their audience through comments, likes, and shares.
2. Establish relationships: Reach out to potential influencers through direct messages or email to discuss collaboration opportunities. Offer something of value in exchange for promotion, such as free products or monetary compensation.
3. Create engaging content: Work closely with the influencer to develop captivating videos that promote your brand or product effectively. These collaborations should be authentic and resonate with both the influencer's style and your desired message.
4. Amplify visibility: Encourage the influencer to share these collaborations on their other social media platforms to maximize visibility outside of TikTok.
5. Track performance metrics: Monitor engagement levels, conversions, and sales generated from these collaborations using analytics tools provided by TikTok or through third-party tracking software.

By leveraging the power of influential individuals on TikTok, you can significantly increase brand awareness, engagement, and ultimately generate income on this exciting platform.

Monetizing your TikTok account: Exploring different income streams

Exploring different income streams

1. Influencer marketing partnerships

One way to monetize your TikTok account is through influencer marketing partnerships. Brands are eager to collaborate with popular TikTok creators who have a large following and can help promote their products or services. By partnering with brands, you can earn money through sponsored content, brand deals, and affiliate marketing.

2. Selling merchandise and products

If you have a loyal fanbase on TikTok, selling merchandise and products can be a lucrative income stream. Whether it's branded t-shirts, stickers, or even your own product line, offering exclusive items related to your TikTok content can attract dedicated followers who want to support you while also representing your brand.

3. Live streaming gifts and donations

Another potential source of income on TikTok is live streaming gifts and donations from your viewers. During live broadcasts, viewers have the option to send virtual gifts as tokens of appreciation or make direct donations using in-app features like "Donation Stickers." Engaging with your audience during these sessions and providing them with unique experiences can encourage them to contribute financially.

With these diverse income streams available on TikTok, creators have the opportunity to turn their passion into a profitable venture while engaging with their audience in creative ways.

Partnering with brands: How to secure lucrative sponsorship deals

Partnering with Brands: How to Secure Lucrative Sponsorship Deals

Building your personal brand on TikTok can open doors for lucrative partnership opportunities with brands. Here are some steps to secure sponsorship deals:

1. **Develop a compelling niche**: Find an area of expertise or interest that sets you apart, allowing brands to see the value in partnering with you.
2. **Grow an engaged audience**: Focus on creating high-quality content consistently and engaging with your followers to build a loyal and active community.
3. **Research relevant brands**: Identify companies that align with your niche and target audience, ensuring their values resonate with yours.
4. **Approach potential partners**: Craft personalized pitches outlining how collaborating would benefit both parties, showcasing the unique advantages of working together.
5. **Showcase your stats and influence**: Present data about your follower count, engagement rate, and reach to demonstrate the impact you can have on a brand's marketing efforts.
6. **Negotiate mutually beneficial terms**: Discuss compensation arrangements such as flat fees or revenue-based partnerships while considering the deliverables expected from each party.

7.**Deliver exceptional results**: Ensure that sponsored content maintains authenticity while delivering value for both brand partners and followers alike.

Selling products and services: Setting up an online store on TikTok

Setting up an Online Store on TikTok

- Selling products and services on TikTok has never been easier.

- By setting up an online store, businesses can leverage the platform's massive user base to generate income.

- Start by creating a business account and optimizing your profile with relevant information and appealing visuals.

- Utilize TikTok's built-in features like shoppable links, product catalogs, and promotional videos to showcase your offerings.

- Engage with your audience through interactive content like live streams and challenges to build brand loyalty.

- Effective marketing strategies include collaborating with popular influencers or running paid ads to reach a wider audience. Overall, TikTok provides a unique opportunity for businesses to sell products and services directly on the platform, reaching millions of users worldwide.

Crowdfunding and donations: Harnessing the power of your fanbase

Crowdfunding and Donations

One innovative way to generate income on TikTok is through crowdfunding and donations. This involves harnessing the power of your fanbase by asking them to contribute funds towards a specific project or cause.

- Encourage support: You can create engaging content that shares your goals or dreams, inspiring your followers to donate towards making them a reality. By expressing genuine gratitude for their support, you can foster a sense of community and loyalty among your fanbase.

- Provide incentives: Consider offering exclusive rewards or perks to those who donate, such as shoutouts in videos, personalized messages, or behind-the-scenes access. These incentives can motivate fans to contribute more generously while also deepening their connection with you.

By tapping into the generosity of your TikTok fanbase through crowdfunding and donations, you have the potential to turn mere viewers into active participants in helping you achieve your goals. Remember to always communicate transparently with your followers about where the donated funds are being allocated, building trust and accountability within this innovative income-generating approach on TikTok.

Becoming a TikTok consultant: Offering your expertise to others

Becoming a TikTok Consultant: Offering Your Expertise to Others

If you have mastered the art of creating engaging content on TikTok, consider becoming a consultant and sharing your expertise with others. Here's how you can leverage your skills to generate income:

1. **Identify your niche:** Determine which aspect of TikTok you excel in, such as dance routines, comedic sketches, or beauty tutorials. Specializing will help establish credibility and attract clients who value your specific knowledge.
2. **Create a portfolio:** Compile examples of your successful TikTok videos and highlight any collaborations or notable achievements. A strong portfolio will demonstrate your abilities and convince potential clients of the value you can bring to their projects.
3. **Offer personalized services:** Tailor consultation packages based on client needs, providing guidance on content creation strategies, optimizing video performance through hashtags and trends analysis, or advising on audience engagement techniques.

Remember that building a reputation as a knowledgeable consultant takes time and dedication - continue staying informed about the latest trends and updates within the platform by actively participating in TikTok communities online to maintain an edge in this ever-evolving space.

Hosting live events and workshops: Engaging with your audience in real-time

Live events and workshops on TikTok allow you to connect directly with your audience. These interactive sessions provide a valuable opportunity to showcase your expertise while building a loyal fan base. During these live events, you can demonstrate how to use specific products or share personal stories that resonate with viewers.

With TikTok's live feature, you can engage in real-time conversations through comments and direct messages. This instant feedback allows for genuine interactions that create a sense of community among your followers. By hosting regular live events and workshops, you can establish yourself as an authority in your niche while cultivating deeper connections with your audience.

Key points:

- Live events and workshops enable direct interaction with TikTok users.
- Showcasing expertise helps build trust and loyalty.
- Instant feedback fosters a sense of community.

Joining TikTok creator programs: Taking advantage of exclusive opportunities

Joining TikTok Creator Programs: Taking Advantage of Exclusive Opportunities

TikTok offers several creator programs that provide exclusive opportunities to its users. By joining these programs, creators can take their content to the next level and generate income in innovative ways.

1. **TikTok Creator Fund**: The TikTok Creator Fund is a program designed to financially support active creators on the platform. It provides them with monetary compensation for their engaging videos and helps them turn their passion into profit.
2. **Brand Partnerships**: Through brand partnerships, TikTok creators can collaborate with well-known brands and promote their products or services in exchange for compensation. These partnerships not only offer financial benefits but also help boost the visibility and credibility of creators.
3. **Supportive Communities**: TikTok also provides various communities where like-minded creators can come together, share ideas, and support each other's growth. These communities often organize meetups or collaborations, enabling partners to learn from one another and expand their reach within the app.

By taking advantage of these exclusive opportunities offered by TikTok, content creators have an incredible chance to monetize their skills while enjoying a creative outlet on this popular social media platform.

Diversifying your income: Exploring cross-platform promotion and beyond

One way to maximize your earning potential on TikTok is by exploring cross-platform promotion. By leveraging the popularity of other social media platforms such as Instagram, YouTube, or Twitter, you can reach a wider audience and increase your chances of monetizing your TikTok content. Consider creating teasers or exclusive content that directs viewers to your other platforms where you can further engage with them.

Another innovative way to generate income on TikTok is through brand partnerships and sponsored content. As your following grows, brands may approach you for collaborations or paid promotions. Make sure to carefully consider which brands align with your values and niche before endorsing their products or services.

Finally, don't limit yourself to just advertising revenue or brand partnerships. Get creative with additional revenue streams like merchandise sales, online courses, or even offering personalized video shoutouts for fans who are willing to support you financially. Diversify your sources of income so that you're not solely reliant on one platform for financial stability.

Analyzing TikTok analytics: Using data to optimize your performance

- Understanding your audience: By analyzing TikTok analytics, you can gain valuable insights into who your viewers are. You'll be able to see their age range, gender distribution, and even their location. This information allows you to tailor your content specifically to the preferences of your target demographic.

- Tracking engagement metrics: Monitoring key engagement metrics such as likes, comments, shares, and views will help you gauge how well your content is resonating with users. This data can guide you in creating more engaging and relevant videos that have a higher chance of going viral.

- Identifying trending hashtags and challenges: TikTok analytics also provide data on popular hashtags and challenges within the platform. By capitalizing on these trends, you increase the visibility of your videos and attract a larger audience. Regularly checking these insights allows you to stay up-to-date with the latest viral trends and adapt your content accordingly.

By leveraging TikTok's robust analytics features effectively, creators can optimize their performance by catering to their target audience's preferences while keeping up with the latest trends on the platform

Protecting your content and brand: Understanding copyright and trademark laws

One essential aspect of utilizing TikTok to generate income is protecting your original content and brand from unauthorized use or infringement. Copyright and trademark laws play a crucial role in safeguarding your creative work and distinctive identity on the platform.

Copyright law

Copyright protects original creative works, such as videos, music, images, or text that you produce for your TikTok account. When you create something unique, copyright automatically grants you exclusive rights to reproduce, distribute, display, perform, and modify that work. To ensure others don't infringe upon your rights:

- Consider adding copyright notices (©) or watermarks to clearly indicate ownership.

- Actively monitor for any instances of unauthorized copying or usage of your content.

- If someone uses your work without permission, reach out to them directly requesting they remove it or consider contacting a legal professional if necessary.

Trademark law

Trademarks are used to protect brands—the names, logos, slogans—that distinguish products or services in the marketplace. Establishing a strong recognizable brand can help increase engagement with potential customers on TikTok. Here's how trademark laws can benefit you:

- Registering trademarks through governmental agencies offers stronger protection against infringement.

- Conduct regular searches within TikTok's platform to detect potential misuse of similar marks that could confuse viewers.

- In case anyone tries impersonating or diluting your brand's reputation on TikTok intentionally seek legal remedies if communication fails.

Remember that understanding these vital intellectual property laws allows you not only to assert ownership over your creative endeavors but also ensures an enjoyable experience for both creators and viewers within the TikTok community.

Overcoming challenges and setbacks: Staying resilient in the TikTok world

Building a successful presence on TikTok comes with its fair share of challenges and setbacks. However, by staying resilient and adopting a few key strategies, users can overcome these obstacles and continue on their path to generating income on the platform.

- Recognize that growth takes time: Building a substantial following on TikTok is not an overnight process. It requires consistency in posting high-quality content, engaging with your audience, and actively participating in trends. Understanding that success may take time will help you stay motivated during slower periods of growth.

- Embrace experimentation: The ever-evolving nature of social media platforms means constantly adapting to new trends, challenges, and algorithm updates. Experimenting with different video formats, editing techniques, or niche topics can help keep your content fresh and appealing to viewers. Don't be afraid to try new things; failure is often just an opportunity for learning and improvement.

- Seek support from the community: The TikTok community is known for being supportive and collaborative. Engage with fellow creators by commenting on their videos, collaborating on duets or stitching their content into yours. By fostering connections within the community, you can gain valuable insights, receive feedback from peers who have faced similar challenges before you.

Remember that setbacks are inevitable but can be turned into opportunities for growth if approached with resilience and adaptability while utilizing the resources available within the TikTok ecosystem

Networking and collaborating with other creators: Growing your TikTok community

Networking and collaborating with other creators

- Collaborating with other TikTok creators can help you expand your reach and grow your community. Reach out to creators who have a similar target audience or content style and propose collaboration ideas.

- Joining creator groups or communities can give you access to valuable networking opportunities. These groups often organize challenges, shoutouts, or collaborations that can expose your content to a wider audience.

- Engage with other creators by liking, commenting, and sharing their videos. Building relationships with fellow TikTokers not only helps increase your visibility but also creates a supportive network within the platform.

The power of cross-promotion

- Cross-promoting on various social media platforms is an effective way to boost your TikTok presence. Share links to your TikTok profile in the bio or description of your Instagram, Twitter, YouTube channels, etc., encouraging followers from these platforms to check out your TikTok content.

- Participate in popular trends and challenges as they emerge on different platforms using hashtags related to those trends.

This can attract users from outside of TikTok who may become interested in exploring more of your content on the platform.

Leveraging duets for collaboration

● Duets allow you to collaborate directly with another creator by singing along, performing alongside them, or reacting/ responding creatively to their video. Participating in duets not only shows support for fellow creators but also exposes you to their existing fanbase.

● When choosing a video for a duet collaboration, make sure it complements both yours and the other creator's content styles. This will help create cohesive content that resonates well with both audiences.

Staying up-to-date with TikTok updates and algorithm changes

• Stay in the loop: To maximize your earning potential on TikTok, it's crucial to stay informed about the platform's latest updates and algorithm changes. Regularly check official sources like the TikTok blog or follow reputable social media experts who share insights on these advancements.

• Adaptability is key: As a creator, being adaptable is vital as TikTok's algorithm evolves over time. Keep track of any noticeable shifts in content trends or engagement patterns to adjust your strategy accordingly. Experimenting with different formats, hashtags, and posting times can give you an edge in reaching new audiences.

• Engage with fellow creators: Collaborating and engaging with other influencers not only enhances your visibility but also keeps you updated about any significant changes happening within the community. Networking through comments, duets, and collaborations can help you gain insights while building valuable relationships that may lead to future opportunities for monetization.

Inspiring success stories: Real-life examples of TikTok users who have unlocked the platform's income potential

Inspiring Success Stories: Real-Life Examples of TikTok Users Who Have Unlocked the Platform's Income Potential

1. ### From Hobby to Hustle: Jasmine's Fitness Journey

Jasmine, a dedicated fitness enthusiast, decided to share her workout routines and healthy meal ideas on TikTok. With engaging content and consistent uploads, she quickly amassed a following of over 100k followers. Capitalizing on her growing popularity, Jasmine collaborated with fitness brands for sponsored videos and even launched her own line of workout apparel. Through strategic monetization efforts, Jasmine now earns a substantial income from her passion for health and wellness.

2. ### Cementing Success through DIY Art: Michelle's Story

Michelle discovered an untapped market as she showcased her DIY art projects on TikTok. Combining creativity with step-by-step tutorials in short videos became Michelle's winning formula, attracting thousands of views and followers. Soon enough, businesses began reaching out to collaborate with Michelle for product promotions and commission-based art projects. Today, Michelle has turned her once hobby into a thriving business that sustains both herself and supports other aspiring artists within the online community.

3. ### Empowering Entrepreneurs: Justin's E-commerce Triumph

Seeking innovative ways to promote his e-commerce business selling environmentally friendly products, Justin found success by utilizing TikTok as his marketing tool of choice. By crafting visually stunning videos showcasing his sustainable products in everyday scenarios while intertwining educational messages about their benefits for the environment, Justin gained traction among environmentally conscious consumers on the platform. As sales skyrocketed thanks to increased brand exposure through viral videos shared by enthusiastic users who resonated with his mission-driven approach, Justin was able to expand his business operations beyond what he initially thought possible.

These stories serve as testament not only to the vast potential TikTok holds for individuals seeking income generation but also its ability to foster communities centered around passions and interests that thrive in a digital era. By maximizing the platform's features and tapping into an engaged audience, TikTok users can unleash their creativity and pave the way for meaningful financial successes.

The Ultimate Guide: Expert Tips on Crafting Viral TikTok Videos

In today's fast-paced digital age, social media platforms continue to redefine the way we consume and create content. Among these new frontiers lies TikTok, a video-sharing app that has taken the world by storm. With its unique blend of short-form videos and quirky challenges, TikTok has emerged as a breeding ground for viral sensations. However, crafting a viral TikTok video is easier said than done. To unlock the secrets behind capturing the attention of millions and amassing followers overnight, we have curated an ultimate guide filled with expert tips from seasoned TikTokers. Whether you're an aspiring creator or simply looking to enhance your online presence, this comprehensive guide will provide you with insights on conceptualization, scripting techniques, editing hacks, sound selection strategies - everything you need to unleash your creativity and increase your chances of going viral on TikTok. Join us as we delve into this exciting realm where innovation meets entertainment; our experts will share their proven strategies for success while reflecting upon those tried-and-failed attempts that ultimately paved their path towards becoming influencers on the platform. Get ready to discover game-changing techniques that are guaranteed not only to elevate your content but also capture hearts globally. So if you're ready to revolutionize your TikTok journey and leave viewers wanting more with each flick of their thumb – then hold onto your seats! As we embark on this adventure together armed with invaluable advice from some of TikTok's most influential voices, let's learn how to ignite moments of brilliance in every 15-second clip and ascend towards stardom in the mesmerizing universe of viral videos!

Understanding the TikTok Algorithm: How to Get Your Video on the "For You" Page

TikTok's algorithm determines which videos appear on users' "For You" page, making it a vital element in achieving virality. To optimize your chances of landing on this coveted page, you need to understand how the algorithm works and tailor your content accordingly.

1. Engage with Trending Hashtags:

Using popular and relevant hashtags can increase the visibility of your TikTok video. Keep an eye on trending topics within your niche and integrate those hashtags into your captions or video descriptions.

2. Create High-Quality Content:

The TikTok algorithm prioritizes videos with high-quality production value, so invest time in creating visually appealing and well-edited videos that captivate viewers from the start.

3. Capture Attention in First Seconds:

Grabbing users' attention is crucial for success on TikTok, as engagement within the first few seconds greatly impacts how extensively your video gets shown. Use catchy hooks or compelling visuals to quickly capture interest.

By understanding these key factors influencing the TikTok algorithm, you can strategically create viral-worthy content that stands out amidst the vast sea of videos, increasing your chances of getting featured on users' "For You" pages.

Finding Your Niche: Discovering Your Unique Voice on TikTok

Finding Your Niche: Discovering Your Unique Voice on TikTok

Explore your interests and passions

To find your niche on TikTok, start by exploring your own interests and passions. Consider what topics you enjoy talking about or creating content around. Whether it's fashion, cooking, comedy, or music, choosing a niche that aligns with your genuine interests will help you create engaging and authentic videos.

Study successful creators in similar niches

Take time to study successful creators who have established themselves in similar niches. Observe their content style, the topics they cover, and how they engage with their audience. This will give you insights into what works well within your chosen niche while also helping you identify gaps where you can offer something unique.

Experiment and refine your approach

Once you've identified your niche, it's important to experiment with different types of content within that space. Try out various video formats, editing techniques, and storytelling approaches to see what resonates best with your audience. Pay attention to the feedback and engagement you receive for each video as this will guide you in refining your approach over time.

Remember that finding success on TikTok takes consistency and patience. Don't be afraid to try new things and adapt as needed along the way!

The Power of Trends: How to Jump on Viral Challenges and Ride the Wave

Trends are unpredictable yet extremely powerful in the world of TikTok. By keeping a close eye on emerging challenges and viral hashtags, you can position yourself to ride the wave of popularity. Joining trending challenges not only increases your chances of going viral but also helps you connect with a wider audience.

To jump on trends effectively, it's crucial to act quickly. Pay attention to popular themes or dance routines that gain traction on TikTok – these are often short-lived opportunities. Once you identify a trend, put your own twist on it while staying true to its essence. Bringing creativity and originality will make your content stand out amidst the competition.

Engaging with other users who participate in trends is equally vital. Collaborate with fellow creators by duetting their videos or joining forces for joint challenges. This expands your reach and forms valuable connections within the TikTok community. Networking through collaboration can lead to mutually beneficial relationships and increased exposure for everyone involved.

Remember, while trends have immense potential, they're fleeting as well! Stay updated about new challenges by following relevant accounts or monitoring popular hashtags regularly. Plan ahead so that when an opportunity arises, you're prepared to create compelling content that resonates with viewers around the globe.

Perfecting Your Opening: Grabbing Attention in the First Few Seconds

Capturing Attention from the Start

Want your TikTok video to go viral? It all starts with a captivating opening that grabs viewers' attention in the first few seconds. This crucial moment can make or break your chances of going viral, so it's important to get it right.

Keep It Short and Snappy

In our fast-paced digital age, attention spans are shorter than ever. To keep viewers hooked from the start, aim for an opening that is short and snappy. Avoid lengthy introductions or slow build-ups; instead, jump straight into the action or grab their interest with a surprising statement or hook.

Create Visual Impact

TikTok is a visually-driven platform, so make sure your opening creates an instant impact through eye-catching visuals. Whether it's bright colors, interesting props, or unique camera angles, find ways to immediately capture viewers' attention visually. Remember, you have just a few seconds to leave a lasting impression before they scroll past.

The Art of Storytelling: Engaging Viewers with Compelling Narratives

Crafting a viral TikTok video requires mastering the art of storytelling. The key is to create compelling narratives that capture the viewer's attention from the very beginning.

1. Start strong: Begin your TikTok video with a hook or an intriguing question that immediately piques curiosity.
2. Keep it concise: Short videos are all the rage on TikTok, so make every second count! Trim unnecessary details and focus on conveying your story in a succinct manner.
3. Emphasize emotions: Connect with your audience by evoking emotions through your storytelling. Whether it's humor, sadness, surprise, or joy, striking an emotional chord enhances engagement and encourages viewers to share your video.
4. Use clear visuals: Visuals play a crucial role in capturing people's attention on TikTok. Make sure they are clear and visually appealing to enhance the overall impact of your narrative.
5. Create relatable content: Identify stories or situations that resonate with a wide range of viewers' experiences to establish an instant connection. Relatability helps drive virality as users often share content that they can personally relate to.

Remember, effective storytelling is at the heart of creating viral TikTok videos! By carefully crafting narratives that engage viewers emotionally and visually, you can increase your chances of going viral on this popular social media platform.

Visual Appeal: Enhancing Your Videos with Eye-catching Effects and Filters

Utilize Eye-Catching Effects and Filters

Adding visual effects and filters to your TikTok videos can help enhance their appeal and make them more engaging for viewers. These effects can range from subtle color enhancements to bold, attention-grabbing animations.

Experiment with Different Effects

- Explore the wide array of effects available on TikTok's editing tools.

- Try using popular filters that are trending on the platform.

- Experiment with different settings to find the ones that best complement your video content.

- Remember, less is often more when it comes to adding effects – choose one or two that really enhance your video rather than overloading it with too many distractions.

Emphasize Visual Storytelling

- Focus on creating a cohesive visual narrative by strategically incorporating effects into your videos.

- Use transitions to smoothly guide viewers' attention from one scene or shot to another.

- Highlight important moments by applying special effects like slow motion or freeze-frame options.

By leveraging eye-catching effects and filters, you can elevate the visual appeal of your TikTok videos and capture the attention of a larger audience.

Mastering Transitions: Seamless Cuts and Creative Edits

Smooth transitions are key to creating engaging TikTok videos. By mastering seamless cuts and creative edits, you can captivate your audience and keep them coming back for more.

1. **Seamless cuts**: Cut between shots in a way that feels natural and effortless. Avoid jarring jumps or awkward pauses that can disrupt the flow of your video. Use techniques such as match cuts, where similar elements in consecutive shots help to create a seamless transition.

2. **Creative edits**: Experiment with different editing techniques to add visual interest to your videos. Try using jump cuts, where quick changes between similar frames give the impression of time passing or fast-paced action. Overlay effects like split screens or image overlays can also add a dynamic touch to your content.

Remember, consistency is key when it comes to transitions and edits! Ensure that each cut aligns with the overall style and tone of your video for a cohesive viewing experience.

Take your TikTok videos from ordinary to extraordinary by practicing these masterful transition techniques - watch as engagement soars!

Lighting and Composition: Creating Professional-looking Videos with Basic Equipment

Good lighting is essential for creating professional-looking videos on TikTok, even if you're only using basic equipment. Natural light is often the best option, so try to shoot near a window or outside during daytime hours. If that's not possible, you can use inexpensive ring lights or desk lamps to brighten up your space.

Composition also plays a crucial role in making your videos stand out. The rule of thirds is a simple but effective technique where you divide your frame into three equal parts vertically and horizontally and place key elements along these lines or at their intersections. This helps create balance and adds visual interest to your shots.

Experiment with different angles and perspectives to bring variety to your videos. High-angle shots can make you appear small and vulnerable, while low-angle shots can add drama and make you look powerful. Don't be afraid to get creative – capturing unique viewpoints will help grab viewers' attention as they scroll through their feeds.

Soundtrack Selection: Choosing the Right Music to Amplify Your Message

Music can make or break your TikTok video, so it's crucial to select a soundtrack that complements your message and resonates with your target audience. Here are some expert tips on choosing the perfect music for your viral content:

1. **Understand the mood**: Consider how you want viewers to feel when watching your video. Is it upbeat and energetic, or emotional and heartfelt? The right soundtrack will evoke the desired emotions and enhance the overall impact of your message.
2. **Match the tempo**: Pay attention to the beats per minute (BPM) of a song as it influences pacing in videos. Faster-paced music creates excitement, while slower tempos lend themselves well to more introspective scenes.
3. **Avoid copyright issues**: TikTok provides an extensive library of licensed tracks that you can use freely without worrying about copyright infringement. Alternatively, explore royalty-free platforms where you can find original tunes that won't compromise your creative vision.

Remember, selecting appropriate background music is just as important as crafting compelling visuals – they work together harmoniously to captivate audiences scrolling through their feeds!

Creative Use of Text and Captions: Adding a Punch to Your Videos

- **Crafting Compelling Titles:** Start with an attention-grabbing title that leaves viewers curious. Keep it short, punchy, and relevant.

- **Strategic Placement of Text**: Place your captions in strategic positions to ensure they don't obstruct the subject of your video. Experiment with font styles and sizes for better visibility.

- **Inject Humor or Wit**: Implement catchy one-liners or relatable jokes within your captions to make viewers chuckle. This can amplify engagement and shareability.

- **Use Emojis Sparingly**: Emojis can enhance captions but should be used sparingly so as not to overwhelm or distract from the main content.

- **Add Contextual Information**: Help viewers understand the context by adding brief text explanations. This is particularly helpful for videos involving tutorials or complex concepts.

- **Create Interactive Captions**: Encourage viewers' participation by asking questions or prompting them to interact via comments, likes, or shares.

- **Experiment with Typography Effects**: Utilize text animation features available on TikTok to add dynamic effects, such as fading in/out, sliding in from different directions, etc.

Remember, concise and witty text elements complemented by well-crafted videos will greatly increase your chances of going viral on TikTok!

Leveraging Hashtags: Maximizing Discoverability and Exposure

Hashtags are a powerful tool to increase the discoverability of your TikTok videos. By strategically including relevant hashtags in your captions, you can reach a wider audience and boost exposure for your content.

- Choose popular hashtags: Research the most trending hashtags related to your video's theme or topic. Using these popular tags increases the likelihood that users searching for those topics will come across your video.

- Be specific with niche hashtags: While using popular hashtags is beneficial, it's also essential to include more niche-specific ones. Niche hashtags help you target a specific audience interested in that particular subject matter, increasing engagement and viewership from people genuinely interested in what you have to offer.

- Strike a balance between quantity and relevance: Including too many irrelevant or unrelated hashtags can confuse TikTok's algorithm and harm discoverability. Aim for 4-6 highly relevant and descriptive tags that accurately represent the content of your video.

Remember, leveraging well-researched and carefully chosen hashtags can significantly enhance the visibility of your TikTok videos, making them more likely to go viral among an eager audience.

Collaborations and Duets: Expanding Your Reach through Partnerships

Collaborating with other TikTok creators can greatly enhance your chances of creating a viral video. By combining your talents and audiences, you not only increase the exposure for each participant but also attract new followers who are interested in both creators' content. Here's how to make the most out of collaborations:

1. **Choose the right partner**: Look for TikTok influencers or content creators whose style aligns with yours, ensuring that their audience would be receptive to your content.
2. **Plan together**: Discuss ideas, themes, and any challenges you may face while collaborating to ensure a cohesive final product.
3. **Promote each other**: Cross-promotion is key! Include tags, mentions, or links to one another's profiles in captions or comments sections to encourage viewers from one account to check out the other.

Dueting videos is another powerful strategy on TikTok as it allows you to engage directly with trending content or collaborate indirectly with fellow creators by adding your own twist. Here are some tips for effective duetting:

- Choose viral videos that match your niche or target audience.

- Don't be afraid to put your unique spin on it - add humor, creativity, or react sincerely!

- Respond genuinely when someone duets with one of YOUR videos - this could create an exciting chain reaction among users!

Remember that collaboration brings additional opportunities for growth and exposure; harness its potential wisely!

Engaging with Your Audience: Responding to Comments and Building Community

Once your TikTok video starts gaining traction and receiving comments, it's crucial to engage with your audience.

1. Respond promptly: Reply to comments as soon as possible to show that you value their feedback and participation. A timely response can encourage more interactions and fuel the sense of community surrounding your content.

2. Be genuine: When replying to comments, be authentic and sincere in your responses. Avoid generic or automated replies; instead, personalize each interaction to foster a genuine connection.

3. Encourage conversations: Spark discussions within the comment section by asking open-ended questions related to your video or requesting suggestions for future content. This not only helps build engagement but also gives you valuable insights into what resonates with your audience.

Remember, building a loyal following on TikTok requires actively engaging with viewers through meaningful conversation and fostering a sense of belonging within your community.

The Importance of Consistency: Establishing a Posting Schedule for Long-term Success

Consistency is key when it comes to building and maintaining an audience on TikTok. By establishing a regular posting schedule, you can create anticipation among your followers and keep them engaged with your content. Plan ahead and determine how frequently you will upload new videos – whether it's daily, every other day, or weekly – and stick to that schedule.

Why is consistency so important? Well, the TikTok algorithm favors accounts that consistently produce high-quality content. By regularly posting videos, you increase the chances of your content being seen by more people. Additionally, consistent posting helps establish your brand identity and build trust among viewers. When they know they can rely on you for fresh content at specific times, they are more likely to become loyal followers.

To make sure that you maintain consistency over time, consider these tips:

- Set aside dedicated time for creating and editing videos.

- Use scheduling tools or reminders to help you stay on track.

- Experiment with different types of content while still staying true to your overall theme.

- Engage with your audience by responding to comments and messages promptly.

By following these strategies and sticking to a consistent posting schedule, you'll be well on your way towards long-term success as a TikTok creator!

Analyzing Metrics: Understanding TikTok's Analytics and Tracking Your Performance

Understanding TikTok's Analytics and Tracking Your Performance

TikTok's analytics provide valuable insights into your video performance. Key metrics to track include views, likes, comments, shares, and engagement rate. These metrics can help you understand how your videos are resonating with your audience and determine what type of content performs best.

Here are some tips for analyzing TikTok metrics effectively:

1. Consistently monitor your view count to gauge the reach of your videos and identify viral trends.
2. Pay attention to the number of likes received as an indicator of audience satisfaction with your content.
3. Comments can provide valuable feedback on viewer preferences or areas for improvement.
4. Track the number of shares to see if others are spreading awareness about your videos.
5. Calculate engagement rate by dividing total engagements (likes + comments + shares) by views multiplied by 100 to assess overall audience engagement.

By utilizing these analytics, you can gain meaningful insights into which strategies work best for maximizing visibility and increasing overall engagement on TikTok.

Going Live: Connecting with Your Fans in Real-time

- **Build anticipation**: Before going live, create buzz among your followers by promoting the upcoming event. Tease them with snippets of what they can expect and encourage them to mark their calendars.

- **Prepare engaging content**: Plan ahead and have a structured outline for your live session. Include interactive elements like Q&A sessions or challenges that will keep viewers engaged throughout.

- **Interact with viewers**: Acknowledge your audience's comments and questions during the livestream. Responding directly to individuals not only makes fans feel special but also encourages others to join in on the conversation.

- **Keep it authentic**: Be yourself! Authenticity is key when connecting with fans. Showcasing your true personality will make viewers feel more connected to you, ultimately forming a loyal fan base.

Going live on TikTok allows you to connect with your fans in real-time, creating an intimate experience that fosters genuine connections. By following these tips, you'll be able to cultivate an engaged community of followers who eagerly anticipate your next livestream. So go ahead and press that "Go Live" button – adventure awaits!

Cross-promotion Strategies: Utilizing Other Social Media Platforms to Grow Your TikTok Following

Utilize the power of cross-promotion by leveraging other social media platforms to increase your TikTok following. Here are a few strategies that can help you expand your reach and attract more viewers:

1. **Share links on Instagram and Facebook**: Take advantage of the built-in audience on these platforms by sharing direct links to your TikTok videos in captions or stories. Encourage your followers to check out your content, providing teasers or behind-the-scenes sneak peeks as an incentive.
2. **Collaborate with influencers**: Collaborating with influencers who have large followings across multiple platforms can give you access to their fans. By teaming up for duets or shoutouts, you can introduce your TikTok account to a wider audience and potentially gain new followers.
3. **Create video previews for YouTube**: YouTube is another popular platform where users spend considerable time watching videos. Create compelling previews of your TikTok content, showcasing the highlights and encouraging viewers to visit your profile for more exciting videos.

Remember that consistency is key when utilizing cross-promotion strategies. Regularly promote your TikTok account across different channels while maintaining high-quality content to maximize visibility and engage with potential followers.

Staying Authentic: Building a Genuine Connection with Your Viewers

Building Trust through Authenticity

Authenticity is key when it comes to building a genuine connection with your viewers on TikTok. People are more likely to engage with content that feels real and relatable, so it's important to stay true to yourself and showcase your unique personality. Avoid trying too hard to fit in or imitate others – be confident in being who you are.

Showcasing Your True Self

One effective way to connect authentically with your viewers is by showing vulnerability. Share personal stories, experiences, or challenges that resonate with others. This creates an emotional connection, making people feel like they can relate to you on a deeper level.

Another tip for staying authentic is engaging in two-way communication with your audience. Responding to comments and messages shows that you genuinely care about their thoughts and opinions. Plus, actively listening allows you to understand what resonates with your viewers and further strengthen the relationship.

Remember, building authenticity takes time; it won't happen overnight. Stay consistent in portraying who you truly are and connecting sincerely with your audience – this realness will naturally shine through in your videos!

Tackling Challenges and Overcoming Setbacks: Lessons from TikTok's Top Creators

Embrace the process of trial and error.

TikTok's most successful creators understand that crafting a viral video takes time and experimentation. They are willing to try new ideas, even if it means failing at first. By embracing the process of trial and error, these creators learn what works best for their audience and continually improve their content.

Stay focused on authenticity.

One lesson learned from top TikTok creators is the importance of staying true to yourself. In a world saturated with content, authenticity stands out. These creators showcase their unique personalities and talents in every video, building genuine connections with their audience along the way.

Persevere through setbacks.

No journey to success is without its setbacks, including on TikTok. Top creators have faced challenges such as slow growth or negative feedback but have persevered nonetheless. They've used setbacks as an opportunity to learn, adapt their strategies, and come back stronger than before.

In summary: Becoming a top creator on TikTok requires embracing trial and error techniques while staying authentic throughout your content creation journey. It also entails persevering through setbacks rather than giving up when things get tough or not going according to plan.

The Future of TikTok: Predictions and Trends to Stay Ahead of the Game

The Future of TikTok: Predictions and Trends

With its explosive growth, it's clear that TikTok is here to stay. But what can we expect from this platform in the future? Here are some predictions and trends to help you stay ahead of the game:

- **Augmented reality (AR) effects:** As technology continues to advance, we can anticipate more sophisticated AR effects on TikTok. From interactive filters to virtual try-on experiences, these features will further enhance user engagement and creativity.

- **E-commerce integration:** Given its massive user base, TikTok has become a prime platform for brands to reach potential customers. In the future, we can expect even more seamless e-commerce integration, making it easier for users to discover and purchase products directly within the app.

- **Collaborative duets:** Collaborative content has always been popular on TikTok. Moving forward, we predict an increase in collaborative duets between creators as they find innovative ways to combine their talents and create viral videos together.

- **Personalized recommendations:** With machine learning algorithms at play, personalized content recommendations will become increasingly accurate on TikTok. Users can look forward to a curated feed based on their preferences and interests.

By staying up-to-date with these predicted trends, you'll be well-equipped to create viral videos that resonate with your audience and keep them coming back for more.

Don't miss out!

Visit the website below and you can sign up to receive emails whenever Coloring Ape publishes a new book. There's no charge and no obligation.

https://books2read.com/r/B-A-EUZZ-IKWOC

BOOKS 2 READ

Connecting independent readers to independent writers.

Did you love *Unleashing the Power of TikTok: Discovering Innovative Ways to Generate Income on the Platform*? Then you should read *Email Marketing Mastery: A Hands-On Approach for Small Business Owners*[1] by Coloring Ape!

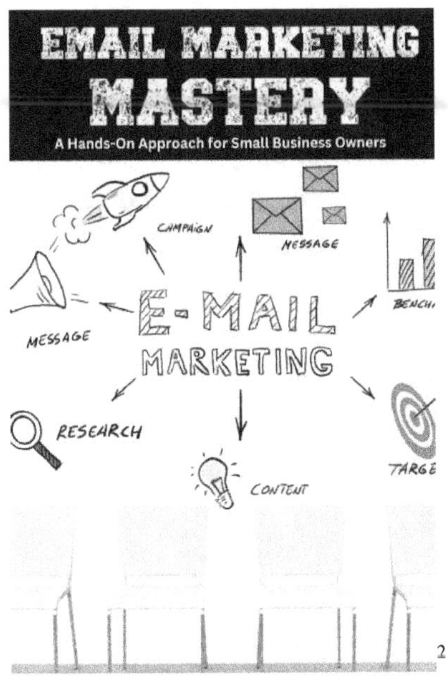

[2]

In today's digital age, email marketing has emerged as one of the most powerful tools for small businesses to connect with their target audience and drive sales. With its ability to reach customers directly in their inbox, email marketing offers a unique opportunity to build relationships, increase brand awareness, and generate valuable leads. In this subchapter, we will delve into the various aspects of email marketing and how it can revolutionize your small business.

First and foremost, we will explore the importance of building an email list. As a small business owner, your email list is your most valuable

1. https://books2read.com/u/brB66Y

2. https://books2read.com/u/brB66Y

asset. It consists of individuals who have willingly shared their contact information and expressed interest in your products or services. We will discuss effective strategies to grow your email list organically, ensuring that you reach the right audience and avoid spamming.

Next, we will dive into the art of crafting compelling email content. A well-crafted email can grab the attention of your recipients, engage them with valuable information, and motivate them to take action. We will provide practical tips and examples to help you create attention-grabbing subject lines, personalized content, and effective calls-to-action. Whether you are sending promotional emails, newsletters, or automated sequences, mastering the art of email content is crucial for success.

Also by Coloring Ape

Email Marketing Mastery: A Hands-On Approach for Small Business Owners
Monetizing Your Passion: How to Turn Your Hobby into a Lucrative Income Stream
Vegan Lifestyle for Pregnant Woman
Unleashing the Power of TikTok: Discovering Innovative Ways to Generate Income on the Platform

www.ingramcontent.com/pod-product-compliance
Lightning Source LLC
Chambersburg PA
CBHW070316160726
47999CB00003B/1042